I Wonder Why

QUESTIONS & ANSWERS ABOUT THE

ANCIENT
WORLD

KING*f*ISHER

KINGFISHER
An imprint of Kingfisher Publications Plc
New Penderel House
283–288 High Holborn
London WC1V 7HZ

Material in this edition previously published by Kingfisher in the
I Wonder Why series.

This edition first published by Kingfisher Publications Plc 1998
10 9 8 7 6 5 4 3 2 1
This edition copyright © Kingfisher Publications Plc 1998

A CIP catalogue record for this book is available from the
British Library.

ISBN 0 7534 0278 5

Printed in Italy

I Wonder Why series:
Editors: Clare Oliver, Brigid Avison, Jackie Gaff, Clare Llewellan
Design: David West Children's Books
Additional design: Smiljka Surla
Art editor: Christiana Fraser

Questions & Answers About the Ancient World:
Assistant Editor: Christian Lewis
Cover design: Mike Smith

Contents

Ancient Egypt

Ancient Greeks

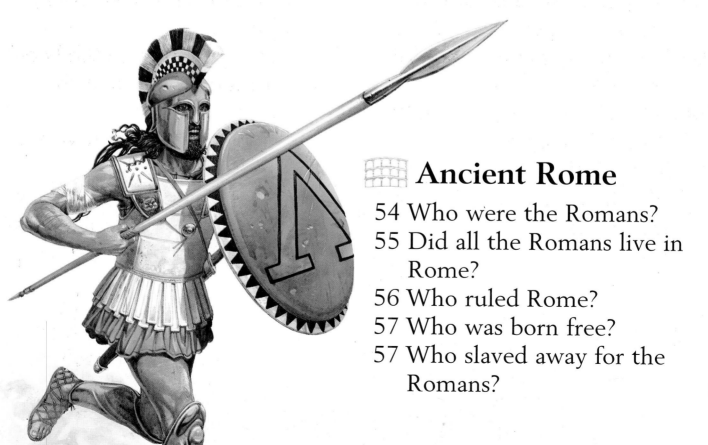

Ancient Rome

Why do we call Egyptians ancient?

We call the Egyptians ancient because they lived such a long time ago – not because they all reached a ripe old age! The first Egyptians were farmers about 8,000 years ago. Within a few thousand years, Egypt had become one of the most powerful countries in the world.

● Will people be studying us in 5,000 years' time? What will they think about the way we live now?

● The Egyptians usually built tombs for dead kings on the river's western bank, where the Sun sets. They believed that their kings went to meet the Sun god when they died.

● Egypt is mostly sandy desert, where nothing grows. The Ancient Egyptians settled on the banks of the river Nile, where there was plenty of water for themselves and their crops.

Ancient Egypt

Why were the Egyptians great?

The Egyptians were so good at farming that they became very rich. They built fantastic temples for their gods, and huge pointed tombs called pyramids where they buried their kings. They had armies and ships and courts of law. Their priests studied the stars and their craftspeople made beautiful things from gold and silver.

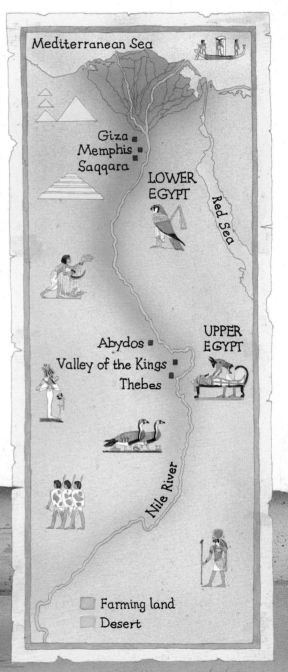

Mediterranean Sea

Giza
Memphis
Saqqara

LOWER
EGYPT

Red Sea

Abydos
Valley of the Kings
Thebes

UPPER
EGYPT

Nile River

Farming land
Desert

Who ruled Egypt?

The king of Egypt was called the pharaoh. The Egyptians believed that their Sun god Re was the first king of Egypt, and that all the pharaohs after him were his relatives. This made the pharaoh very holy – and very powerful! The people thought he was a god on Earth.

● The pharaoh's advisors were called the Honoured Ones. There were all sorts of royal officials, too, with grand names like the Director of Royal Dress and the Keeper of the Royal Wigs.

Could a woman be pharaoh?

Although very few women ruled Egypt, there was a famous pharaoh called Hatshepsut. When her six-year-old nephew came to the throne, Hatshepsut was asked to rule Egypt for him – just until he was a little bit older. But Hatshepsut liked ruling so much that she wouldn't let her nephew take over. He didn't get the chance to rule until he was 30 years old!

● When she was pharaoh, Hatshepsut had to wear the badges of royalty. These included a false beard, made of real hair.

How would you know if you met a pharaoh?

He would be wearing a crown, of course! In fact, pharaohs sometimes wore two crowns at the same time – a white one for Upper Egypt, which was the name for the south of the country, and a red one for Lower Egypt, which was the north.

Who was the crocodile god?

In old paintings and carvings, most Egyptian gods and goddesses have animal heads. The water god, Sebek, was shown as a crocodile. Thoth had the head of a bird called an ibis, while Taweret looked like a hippo! Osiris and Isis were luckier. They were shown as a great king and queen.

● The Egyptians loved to wear lucky charms. Their favourites were scarabs. The scarab beetle was sacred to the Sun god, Re.

● The Ancient Egyptians worshipped as many as 2,000 gods and goddesses!

Thoth, god of learning

Osiris, god of death

Who was the goddess Nut?

Nut was goddess of the heavens and she was usually shown covered in stars. Many gods and goddesses were linked in families. Nut was married to Geb. Isis and Osiris were their children.

● Being a priest was a part-time job. Most only spent 3 months a year at the temple, and lived at home the rest of the time.

BACK IN 9 MONTHS

● Priests had to wash twice during the day and twice at night, to make themselves clean and pure for the gods.

Taweret, goddess of childbirth and babies

Isis, wife of Osiris

11

Why were the pyramids built?

The pyramids were huge tombs for dead pharaohs and other very important people. No one knows exactly why the pyramids were shaped this way. Some people think they were built to point towards the Sun and stars, so that the dead person's spirit could fly to heaven like a rocket.

● The Great Pyramid at Giza was built more than 4,500 years ago. This is what it looks like today.

● Pharaohs were buried with all their finest clothes and jewellery, so tombs were given sneaky traps to catch out robbers.

● There are other, smaller pyramids at Giza, and over 80 at other places in Egypt. Some have stepped sides and bent tops.

● This is what the
Great Pyramid
looks like
inside.

Pharaoh's
chamber

Why did the Egyptians bury their mummies?

A mummy is a dead body which has been dried out so it lasts for thousands of years. The Egyptians believed that the dead travelled to another world, where they needed their bodies. And they didn't want any bits missing!

- Some poorer families had their nearest and dearest mummified, but it was an expensive business. Only the rich could afford a really good send-off.

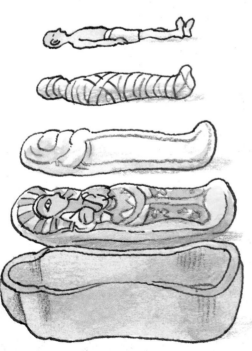

- The mummy was placed inside a series of wooden coffins. These were put in a big stone case called a sarcophagus.

- Monkeys, crocodiles, cats and other sacred animals were often mummified, too!

Why were mummies brainless?

The Ancient Egyptians believed that the heart was the most important part of the whole body. They thought that the brain was useless. So when they were preparing a mummy, they took out the brain – by pulling it down through the nose!

Why were mummies wrapped in bandages?

Wrapping the dead body helped to keep its shape. After the insides were removed, the body was dried out for 40 days in salty stuff called natron. Then it was washed, rubbed with ointments, and tightly bandaged.

Why did people sit on the roof?

The roof was just about the best spot in an Egyptian house. It was cooler than indoors, especially under a shady canopy. People liked to sit and talk there, or play board games.

● Most houses were made of mud bricks, but stone blocks were used for temples, tombs and palaces.

● Egyptian houses had flat roofs. Pointed roofs were invented in rainy lands, to let the water drain away.

Who made mud pies?

Bricks were made from river mud. Brick-makers trampled the mud with their bare feet until it was sticky. They added bits of straw and reed to make the mixture firmer. Then they shaped the mud pies into bricks, which dried hard in the Sun.

Who had nightmares?

Some Egyptians must have slept well, but their beds do look very uncomfortable! They were made of wood, with ropes or leather straps instead of springs. And people didn't lie on soft pillows filled with feathers. All they had were wooden headrests!

Who liked to get knee-deep in mud?

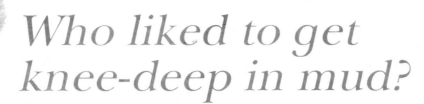

Egyptian farmers loved mud – it has all the water and goodness that plants need to grow well. The most important time in a farmer's year was when the Nile flooded and dumped rich, black mud on the dry fields. A good flood meant a good harvest. A bad one meant people went hungry.

• Priests watched the Moon and stars to work out a calendar of the months. This told them when the floods would come and when to plant crops.

• Juicy grapes and fresh green vegetables were grown in the rich Nile mud. Golden ears of wheat and barley were harvested and stored in granaries.

• The only farm land in Egypt is near the river Nile. It used to be called the Black Land, because the mud left by the floods was black. The rocky desert was called the Red Land.

Which was the fastest way to travel?

The quickest route in Egypt was the river Nile. Egyptian boats were made from river reeds or wood. They were the only way to get from one side of the river to the other – unless you swam and liked crocodiles!

- The big question each year was: "How deep is the flood?" Notched stones were used like giant rulers to measure the rising water. The stones were called nilometers.

- Farmers dug ditches to carry water to their crops when the Nile wasn't in flood. They used a clever machine called a shaduf to lift water out of the river into the ditches.

Who looked really cool?

Egypt is a very hot country, and in ancient times people kept cool by wearing as little as possible. Ordinary workers just wore a simple cloth around their waists. But for the rich, the coolest fashion was graceful clothes made from the finest linen.

● Linen is made from a plant called flax. It's very hard to prepare, but the Egyptians could spin and weave it into lengths of beautifully light and flimsy cloth.

● Acrobats and dancing girls just wore strings of beads!

● Women wore long dresses with shoulder straps. Men wore long kilts that hung in folds. Children often wore nothing at all.

20

Who liked to sparkle?

Most clothes were plain white, so rich people added colour and sparkle by wearing beautiful jewellery made from gold and colourful precious stones.
Sometimes, for a special feast, they wore wide cloth collars decorated with leaves, wildflowers or glass-like beads. Poorer people's jewellery was made from copper and shells.

● Both men and women wore jewellery.

Why did shoes wear out?

Servants' shoes were woven from reeds which they gathered from the river bank. The shoes didn't last long – particularly when the servants had to keep running around after their rich masters and mistresses!

Who played with lions?

Nobody did, if they had any sense! But young children did play with wooden lions and other toy animals. Children also had spinning tops, as well as balls that rattled, and dolls with beads in their hair.

● Few people could read, so after a day's work they probably sat down to listen to storytellers. There were many exciting tales about gods and goddesses.

● Children ran around playing ball-games or tag, then cooled off with a swim in the river.

Who played board games?

Tutankhamun became pharaoh when he was only 12 years old. He loved playing a board game called senet, and after he died a board was buried with him in his tomb. It is a beautiful set, made of white ivory and a black wood called ebony.

● The senet board had 20 squares on one side and 30 on the other. Experts think it was a bit like ludo.

Did Egyptians like parties?

● Musicians plucked harps, beat drums and tambourines, blew pipes and shook tinkling bells.

The Egyptians might have spent a lot of time building tombs, but they weren't a miserable lot! They loved music and dancing. At rich people's banquets, there were often shows with dancing girls, musicians, acrobats and singers.

Why is paper called paper?

Our word 'paper' comes from papyrus, a tall reed that grows beside the Nile. The Egyptians discovered how to use the thready insides of these papyrus reeds to make a kind of paper. It was thicker than the paper we use today, but just as useful.

● Papyrus was expensive because it took so long to make. Quick notes were scribbled on pieces of pottery instead.

1 Paper-makers cut and peeled the reeds.

3 They hammered them until the sticky plant juices glued them together.

4 Next they used a smooth stone or a special tool to rub the surface of the papyrus paper smooth.

24

2 They cut the reed stems into thin slices and then laid them in rows, one on top of the other.

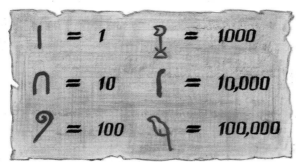

| = 1	⚱ = **1000**
∩ = **10**	𝄢 = **10,000**
𝟗 = **100**	⟜ = **100,000**

● Few children went to school. Some boys trained as scribes, people whose job was writing. They had to learn over 700 hieroglyphs. Spelling tests were a nightmare!

● There were even pictures for numbers. It can't have been easy doing sums!

What did Egyptian writing look like?

5 Finally, all the pieces of papyrus paper were glued into a long strip and rolled into a scroll.

The first Egyptian writing was made up of rows of pictures, called hieroglyphs. Each picture stood for an object, an idea, or the sound of a word. Many of the hieroglyphs are quite complicated – they must have taken ages to draw!

● The ends of reeds were frayed to make paintbrushes. Ink was made from soot or red earth.

● These hieroglyphs make up the name CLEOPATRA. Perhaps you can work out how to write TOP CAT or TREACLE.

C L E O P A T R A

Which were the most dangerous animals?

Egypt wasn't always a safe place. Wild bulls and lions lived in the desert, while hungry crocodiles lurked in the river Nile. Many Egyptians enjoyed hunting these animals, even though they could be dangerous.

● Even hippo-hunting could be dangerous. An angry hippo could easily overturn one of the hunter's tiny boats.

● When it died, a pet dog was buried with its collar – all ready for a walk in the after-life!

Did people have pets?

Rich Egyptians had pets, just as we do today, and they loved them just as much. Most people settled for a dog or a cat, but people who really wanted to show off kept pet apes and monkeys.

● Today there are no lions or hippos left in Egypt. They are only found in countries far to the south. But Ancient Egyptians would still recognize birds such as the ibis and the hoopoe.

● The whole family went along on duck hunts. The birds were brought down by sticks, which were a bit like boomerangs – only they didn't come back!

● Ostriches were hunted for their large tail feathers. These were made into beautiful fans to keep rich people cool.

What did Egyptians call their cats?

The Egyptian word for cat was miw – a cross between a mew and a miaow! The Egyptians were probably the first to tame cats. They used them to catch mice in grain stores.

How can you become an Egyptologist?

Egyptologists are people who study Ancient Egypt. To become one, you need to learn all about the history of Egypt, and the things that have survived from that time. Reading books and visiting museums are the best ways to start.

● Howard Carter went to Egypt in 1892, and spent many years excavating Ancient Egyptian tombs. He made his most famous discovery in 1920 – the tomb of the boy-pharaoh Tutankhamun.

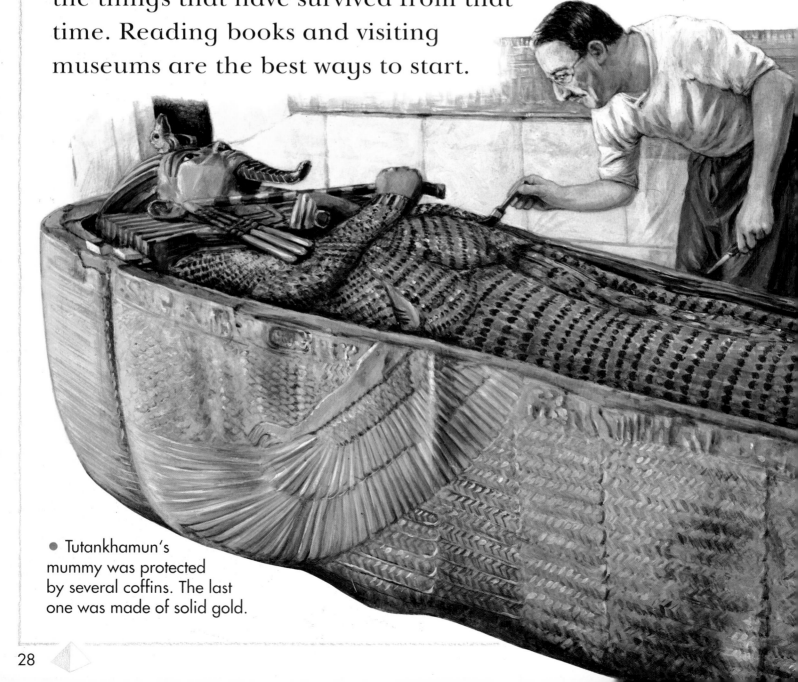

● Tutankhamun's mummy was protected by several coffins. The last one was made of solid gold.

Why do mummies have X-rays?

Modern science is a great help to Egyptologists. X-rays can show whether a mummy died from an illness or an accident. They can even tell whether it suffered from toothache!

● Egyptologists can even run tests on the things they find in a mummy's tummy, and work out what its last meal was before it died!

Where can you come face to face with a pharaoh?

Egypt's largest museum is in the capital city of Cairo. Here, you can gaze on the 4,000-year-old faces of the mummified pharaohs. Not all the pharaohs are here, though. Some are still lying peacefully, hidden in their desert tombs.

Who were the Ancient Greeks?

The Ancient Greeks were people who lived in Greece from around 3,500 years ago. But they didn't live only in Greece. Some lived to the north and the east, in lands that we now call Bulgaria and Turkey. Others lived on small rocky islands in the Aegean Sea.

● Many Greek people set sail for North Africa, Turkey, Italy and France. They found safe harbours, where they built new homes and towns, and cleared the land for farming.

Greek homeland
Greek colonies

FRANCE
ITALY
Mediterranean Sea
NORTH AFRICA
Aegean Sea
TURKEY

● By 500BC the Greek world was large, rich and powerful. It stretched from France in the west to Turkey in the east.

● Wherever they went, the Greek settlers took their own way of life. They must have looked odd to the locals!

Ancient Greece

Why did Greece grow bigger and bigger?

Greece and its homelands were small, and much of its land was too rocky for farming. By about 750BC, there was little room left for new towns or farms, and food began to run short. Because of this, many people left Greece to look for new places to live, and the Greek world began to grow.

Was Greece one big happy country?

Ancient Greece was not a single country like Greece is today. It was made up of different states, which were cut off from each other by high mountains, deep valleys, or the sea. The states weren't much bigger than cities, but they each had their own laws and army, and often quarrelled with each other. Athens was the biggest city-state.

● Each state was made up of a city and the surrounding countryside. Many city-states lay close to the sea, and had a harbour, too.

HARBOUR

TEMPLE

PRISON

AGORA

SCHOOL

CITY WALLS

FARMLAND

Where did the citizens take charge?

- Sparta was a city-state in southern Greece. It was ruled by two kings from two royal families, who were helped by a council of wise old men.

In Athens, all grown men who weren't slaves were citizens. They could choose their government officials and vote for or against new laws. Citizens could also speak at the Assembly. This was a huge open-air meeting where people stood up and told the government what it should be doing.

- There had to be at least 6,000 citizens at every Assembly. They all met on the slopes of a hill in Athens, and voted by raising their hand.

- Most wealthy Greek households had slaves. The slaves did all the hard work, such as building, farming, housework and looking after the children.

Where did the clock go drip-drop?

Citizens who spoke at the Assembly weren't allowed to drone on for too long. Each speaker was timed with a water clock. When the last drop of water had dripped out of the jar, his time was up. He had to sit down and hold his tongue!

Who were the fiercest soldiers?

The soldiers of Sparta were the fiercest army in Ancient Greece. They were brave, ruthless and very well-trained. None of the men had ordinary jobs, even in peacetime. They spent their whole lives just training and fighting.

● Spartan warriors were famous for their long flowing hair. Before a battle, they sat down and combed it. Perhaps their long manes made them feel like lions!

● For Spartans, bravery was more important than anything else. To punish cowards, they shaved off half their hair and half their beard! This was a terrible disgrace.

Who paid for weapons and armour?

● Greek soldiers fought side by side in tight rows called phalanxes. Each soldier's shield overlapped his neighbour's, making a strong wall of shields that protected all of them.

Greek soldiers had to buy their own weapons and armour. A wealthy soldier bought himself a sharp spear and sword, a strong shield, and expensive body armour. But a poor soldier made do with whatever he could find. And sometimes this was little more than an animal skin and a wooden club!

● In Sparta it wasn't just the men who had to be fit. Women had to do lots of exercises to make sure their babies were healthy and strong.

● After winning a battle, soldiers sometimes gave their armour to the gods as a thank-you present. They laid it inside a temple or hung it on the branches of a tree.

Why did ships have long noses?

Greek warships had a long sharp spike at the front. It was called a ram, and in battle it could be deadly. The oarsmen rowed as fast as they could towards an enemy ship and tried to smash a hole in its side with the ram. With any luck, the enemy ship would sink and its crew would all be drowned.

● Most Greek ships had a big eye painted on either side of the prow. The sailors hoped that these staring eyes would frighten away evil spirits, and protect the men until they were safely home.

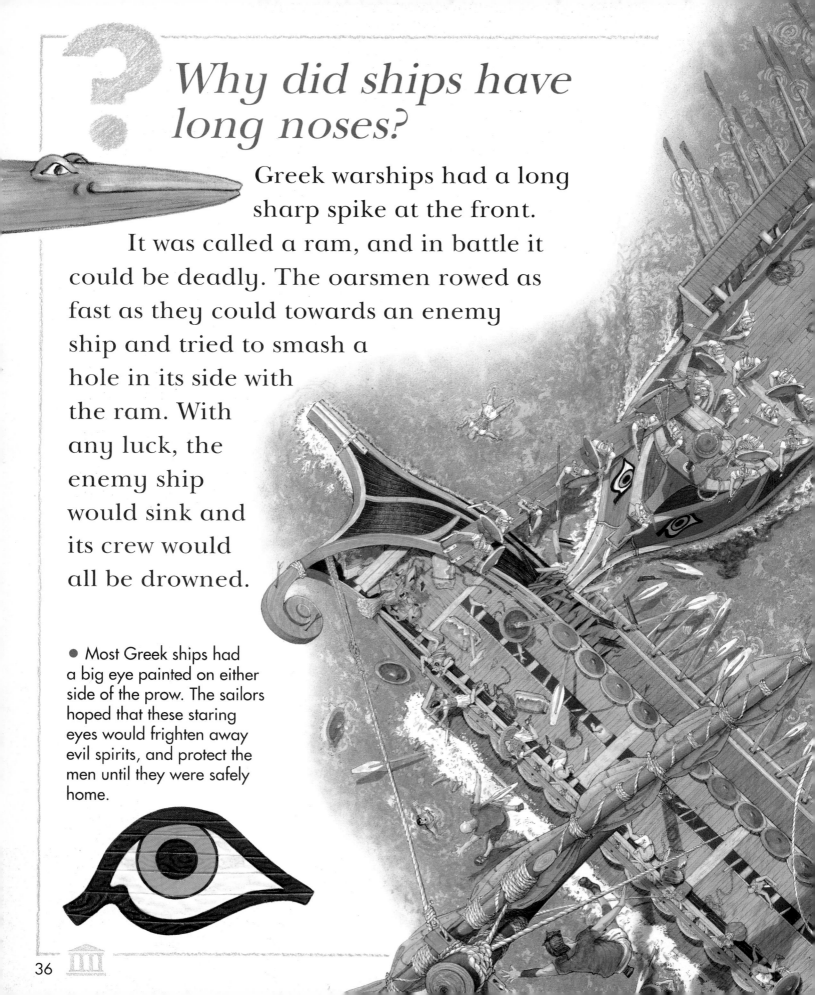

• The biggest warships were called triremes, and had three rows of oarsmen along each side of the boat. With 170 men pulling on the oars, ships zipped through the water at an amazing speed.

• Each ship had a flute-player who piped tunes with a steady beat. The oarsmen all pulled their oars in time with the music, which meant they didn't get all tangled up!

Why was it easier to travel by sea?

There are many islands in Greece and boats are often still the only way to get from one island to another. But the Ancient Greeks used boats to get around the mainland too. Sailing along the coast was much quicker and easier than struggling up steep, stony tracks on the back of a weary donkey!

Who was goddess of wisdom?

Athene was the goddess of war and also of wisdom, and so her symbol was the wise owl. She had special powers to protect the city of Athens. Because of this, the citizens loved and worshipped her. They built Athene her very own temple, the Parthenon, high on the Acropolis, a hill overlooking the city.

● According to stories, the gods lived on top of Mount Olympus, the highest mountain in Greece. But they didn't always behave as you'd expect gods to – they spent a lot of their time quarrelling!

Hermes messenger of the gods

Zeus king of the gods

Demeter goddess of crops

Aphrodite goddess of love and beauty

Hera queen of the gods, goddess of women and children

Hades god of the underworld

● The Greeks believed in many different gods and goddesses. Each one had different powers. Some of the gods were kind, but others were stern and cruel.

Who told stories about the gods?

A famous poet called Homer told many exciting stories about gods and heroes. His long poem *The Odyssey* tells the adventures of Odysseus, a Greek soldier sailing home to Ithaca from the war with Troy. The sea god Poseidon tries to sink his ship, but with Athene's protection, Odysseus finally gets home.

● Inside the Parthenon stood a towering statue of Athene – about ten times taller than you! It was covered with precious gold and ivory.

● Poseidon was god of the sea. He tried to sink Odysseus's ship by stirring up violent storms.

Why did Greeks build temples?

The Greeks built temples as homes for their gods. They made the buildings as magnificent as possible, using only the finest materials and very best craftsmen, so the gods would be pleased. Elegant statues, tall columns and painted friezes decorated the outside. Inside, the rooms were filled with treasures.

● The Parthenon in Athens was built from dazzling white marble. The huge stone blocks were carried to the building site on ox-drawn carts and hauled up to the builders on ropes and pulleys.

Whose fingers made their fortune?

Greek craftsmen were very skilful, and made beautiful works of art. Stonemasons carved marble figures, metalworkers made statues and vases of bronze, while potters and painters made wonderful jars and flasks. Some craftsmen became rich and famous and sold their work abroad as well as at home.

● Greek potters were famous for their beautiful bowls, vases and cups. They worked with artists, who decorated the pottery in red or black, with paintings of heroes, gods or ordinary people.

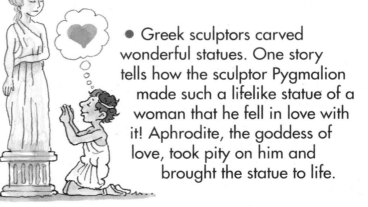

● Greek sculptors carved wonderful statues. One story tells how the sculptor Pygmalion made such a lifelike statue of a woman that he fell in love with it! Aphrodite, the goddess of love, took pity on him and brought the statue to life.

● Temple columns weren't made from one single piece of stone. They were built from drum-shaped pieces held together by pegs. The pieces fitted together snugly – so long as you put them in the right order!

When did a couple get married?

Most couples got married when their parents said so! A wealthy father wanted a good match for his son or daughter – one that would make the family even richer and more important. Greek brides were only 13 or 14 years old when they got married. Their husbands were usually much older – 30, at least.

● On her wedding day, the bride was driven in a chariot to her new husband's home. There was laughter and music, and burning torches to light the way.

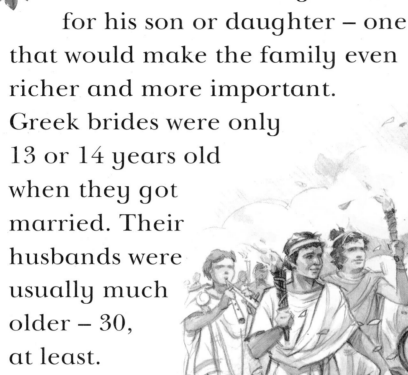

● The bride's chariot was broken after the wedding, as a sign that she could never go back to her old home.

What did girls do all day?

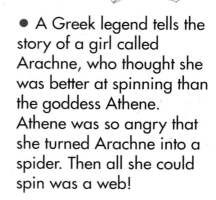

Young girls from wealthy families were sometimes taught to read at home, but girls didn't go to school. Most learnt from their mother how to spin fleece into thread, and then weave it into fine woollen cloth. Greek women made all the cloth their families needed – for wall hangings, blankets and rugs as well as for clothes.

● A Greek legend tells the story of a girl called Arachne, who thought she was better at spinning than the goddess Athene. Athene was so angry that she turned Arachne into a spider. Then all she could spin was a web!

● A few women did learn to read and write. One of the most famous Greek poets was a woman called Sappho, who lived about 2,500 years ago.

Who went to the gym every day?

'Gym' is short for 'gymnasium', the Greek name for school. Boys went to school from about the age of seven. They learnt all the usual things like reading, writing and maths, as well as how to make a speech, recite poetry and sing.

Why were Greek clothes so comfy?

The Greeks wore light, loose-fitting clothes. There were no tight buttons or zips, just flowing robes or simple tunics called chitons (say *kit-owns*). Chitons were just big squares of cloth, draped over the body and held in place by pins at the shoulders and a belt round the waist.

• The Greeks liked brightly-coloured clothes, decorated with embroidery. Most clothes were made out of wool or linen, but rich people wore silk, too.

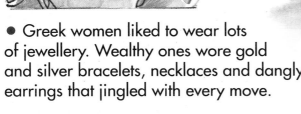

• Greek women liked to wear lots of jewellery. Wealthy ones wore gold and silver bracelets, necklaces and dangly earrings that jingled with every move.

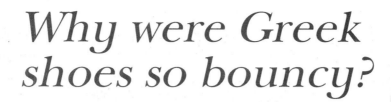

Why were Greek shoes so bouncy?

Most Greeks liked to go barefoot in the house. But when they went out, they wore cool summer sandals or warm winter boots. The comfiest ones had thick soles made of cork. This made them soft and bouncy – just right for walking on stony ground.

● The Greeks wore wide-brimmed hats made of plaited straw to protect themselves from the scorching summer sun.

Who took a shower in a bowl?

When the Ancient Greeks wanted a shower, they stripped off and crouched inside a deep pottery bowl. Then a slave would come and pour jars of cool, refreshing water all over them.

Why did actors wear masks?

In Ancient Greece, only boys and men were actors. They wore masks so that the audience could see what part they were playing – a man or a woman, a wise person or a fool. Greek theatres were huge, with seats for up to 17,000 people. From the back you couldn't have seen the actors' faces, but the big, colourful masks were easy to make out.

● Some plays lasted all day. The audience took cushions and rugs to put on the hard stone seats, and bought snacks and wine when they felt hungry or thirsty.

● Greek theatres stood on sloping hillsides. Their semicircular shape helped carry the actors' voices right to the back – even when they whispered!

How did a tortoise make music?

Sad to say, a tortoise only made music when it was dead. An empty tortoiseshell was used to make a lyre, a musical instrument rather like a harp. Musicians fixed strings to the shell and plucked them to play a tune.

● The double flute was another popular musical instrument but it was difficult to play. You needed twice as much puff as for a single flute, and each hand played a different tune.

● Theatre staff carried big sticks in case of trouble. Sometimes the huge audience got carried away by a play and began to riot. A few hefty whacks soon quietened them down!

Why were the Olympics held?

The Olympic Games were part of a religious festival in honour of Zeus, king of the gods. Every four years, 20,000 people flocked to Olympia to watch athletes run, box, wrestle, and race chariots. The hardest event of all was the pentathlon. Contestants had to take part in five different sports – the long jump, running, wrestling, throwing the discus and throwing the javelin.

● Women were banned from the Olympics. They held their own games, in honour of Hera, queen of the gods. The women's games had only one event, which was running.

● At the Olympics all the athletes were naked. The Greeks were proud of their bodies, and weren't afraid to show them off!

Did the winners get medals?

Winning at the Olympics was a great honour, just as it is today. But there were no medals in the ancient games. Instead, the winners got crowns made of laurel leaves, jars of olive oil, beautiful pots or vases, and pieces of wool, silk or linen to make into clothes.

● Greek boxers didn't wear padded gloves like boxers today. They simply wrapped strips of leather around their fists.

Who ran the first marathon?

In 490BC the Greeks won a battle at Marathon, about 42 kilometres from Athens. A Greek soldier called Pheidippides ran all the way to Athens to tell the citizens the good news. Sadly, his 'marathon' exhausted him, and the poor man collapsed and died.

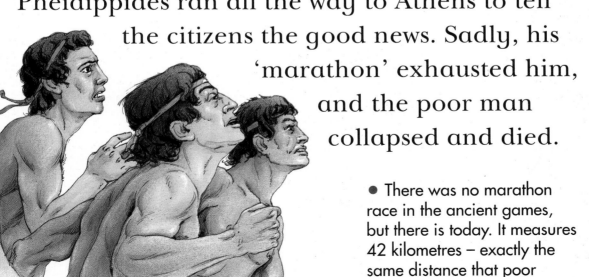

● There was no marathon race in the ancient games, but there is today. It measures 42 kilometres – exactly the same distance that poor Pheidippides ran 2,500 years ago.

Why did doctors ask so many questions?

Greek doctors knew it was important to find out as much as they could about their patients. So they asked them all sorts of questions – what sort of food they ate, whether they took any exercise, and so on. People had once believed illness was a punishment from the gods, but Greek doctors had more scientific ideas.

● Greek doctors were clean, well-dressed and cheerful. It made their patients trust them and the doctors knew this helped people to get better more quickly.

Who had his best ideas in the bath?

Archimedes was a mathematician who lived in Greece around 250BC. One day when he was in the bath, he finally worked out a problem that had been troubling him for ages. He was so excited he jumped out of the bath shouting 'Eureka!' ('I've got it!'), and ran down the street to tell his friends!

• The Greeks loved learning about new ideas. They would sit under a shady tree and talk for hours about all sorts of things, from the way people lived to the future of the world.

Who discovered that the Earth is round?

Greek scientists were very interested in the Earth and space. In about 470BC, a scientist called Parmenides was watching an eclipse of the Moon. He noticed the Earth cast a dark, curved shadow on the Moon, and worked out that if the shadow was curved then the Earth must be round!

• One famous Greek thinker was called Diogenes. He lived in an old wooden barrel so people could see that he didn't care about money or possessions. He was only interested in ideas.

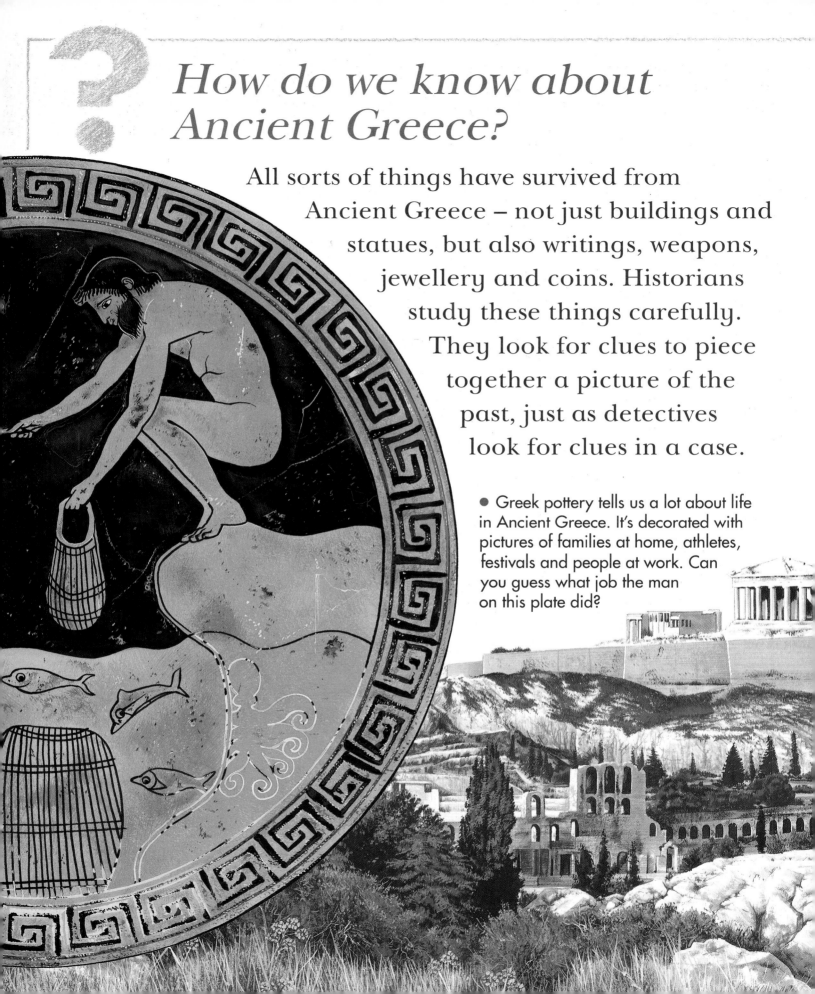

How do we know about Ancient Greece?

All sorts of things have survived from Ancient Greece – not just buildings and statues, but also writings, weapons, jewellery and coins. Historians study these things carefully. They look for clues to piece together a picture of the past, just as detectives look for clues in a case.

● Greek pottery tells us a lot about life in Ancient Greece. It's decorated with pictures of families at home, athletes, festivals and people at work. Can you guess what job the man on this plate did?

- The Greek world began to break up around 300BC. In Italy the Romans were growing stronger. They invaded Greece in 148BC and soon took control.

Who copied the Greeks?

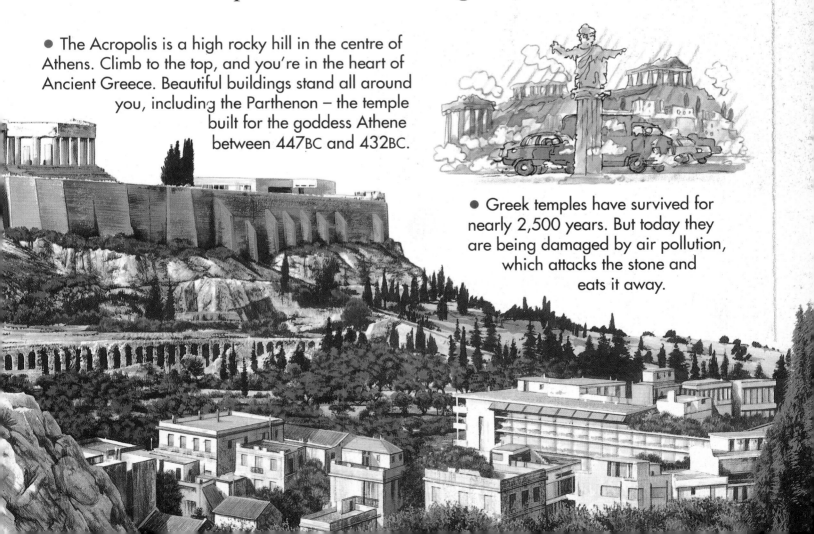

About 2,000 years ago, the Romans marched into Greece. They conquered its armies and added its lands to their own empire. But Roman people respected the Greek way of life. They admired Greek poetry, plays, buildings and art. They copied many Greek ideas and used them to improve their own way of life.

- The Acropolis is a high rocky hill in the centre of Athens. Climb to the top, and you're in the heart of Ancient Greece. Beautiful buildings stand all around you, including the Parthenon – the temple built for the goddess Athene between 447BC and 432BC.

- Greek temples have survived for nearly 2,500 years. But today they are being damaged by air pollution, which attacks the stone and eats it away.

Who were the Romans?

The Romans were people who came from Rome. About 2,000 years ago they became so powerful that they began to conquer the lands around them. By AD100 they ruled a huge empire, and were one of the mightiest peoples in the ancient world.

● Different parts of the empire had very different climates. Romans boiled in Egypt, where the summers were sweltering...

● An old legend says that the city of Rome was first started by a man called Romulus. He and his twin brother Remus had been abandoned by their parents and looked after by a wolf!

● ...but they shivered in the icy Swiss Alps and in northern Britain. These were the coldest places in the whole empire.

Ancient Rome

● There were about 50 million people in the Roman empire. It stretched from Britain in the north to Africa in the south. Everyone in the empire was protected by Rome's armies, but had to obey Rome's laws.

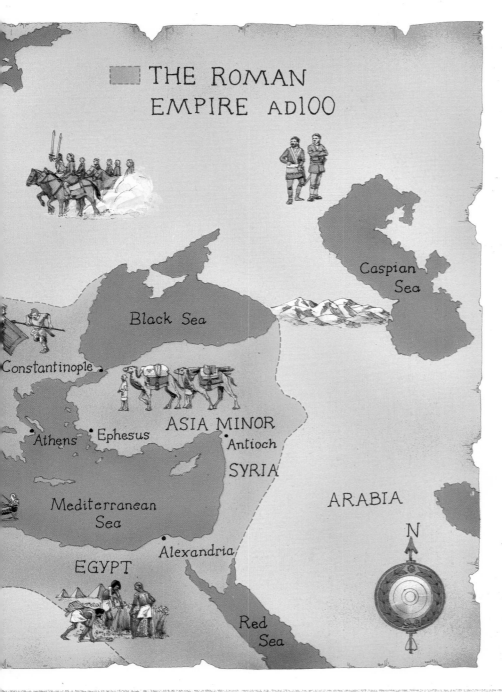

THE ROMAN EMPIRE AD100

Caspian Sea

Black Sea

Constantinople

Athens   Ephesus   ASIA MINOR
                      Antioch
                      SYRIA

Mediterranean Sea   ARABIA   N

Alexandria

EGYPT   Red Sea

● It would have taken nearly 100 days to ride from one end of the empire to the other. It was a journey of over 3,000 Roman miles, about 5,000 kilometres.

Who ruled Rome?

Over the years, Rome was ruled in three different ways: first by kings, then by a number of officials who were chosen by the people, and finally by emperors, who were really kings under a different name!

● Some Roman emperors ruled wisely, but others did whatever they pleased...

Nero was mad and bad. Some people say he set fire to the city of Rome.

Hadrian visited every corner of the empire, and made it stronger.

Caligula wasted the riches of Rome. He believed he was a god.

Who was born free?

Roman citizens. They were not only able to vote in elections, they also got free seats at the amphitheatre and free use of the public baths. When times were hard, they got free loaves of bread, too!

● Roman women did not have the same rights as men. They were not allowed to vote, and had to obey their husband or father. But that doesn't mean they always did!

Who slaved away for the Romans?

Most of the hard work in Rome was done by slaves. These men, women and children were captured abroad, and then sold in the marketplace in Rome. They had to wear an identity tag with their master's name and address on it – just in case they got lost.

● The first Roman emperor was called Augustus. He was advised by a group of wealthy men, called senators, who were used to running the army and the government.

● Slaves were sometimes given their freedom after many years of good service, or if their master wanted to be kind.

When did the army use tortoises?

When Roman soldiers were advancing towards the enemy, they did a special trick called 'the tortoise'. They held their shields high above their heads to make a sort of shell. This protected them from enemy spears – but made it hard for them to see where they were going!

Dear Mum
Having an awful time.
The Barbarians are fierce and I think the Centurion hates me.
Please send V sesterces for food.
Your loving son
Marcus XXX

● Soldiers were often hungry and cold. Many of them wrote letters home asking for extra food and clothing.

● Injured soldiers bandaged their wounds with cobwebs soaked in vinegar. This helped the soldiers, but wasn't so good for the spiders!

Which soldiers left home for 25 years?

Most soldiers had to stay in the army for 25 years. Those who were Roman citizens were luckier – they could leave after just 20 years! Soldiers had a hard life. They were far from home, and had to put up with danger, tough training and harsh punishments.

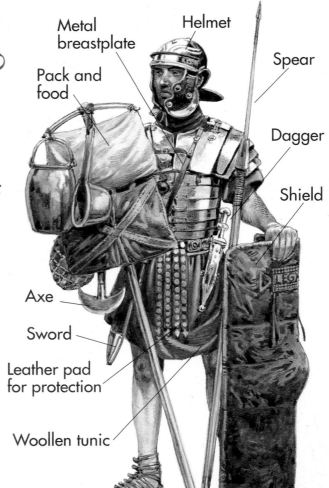

Metal breastplate

Helmet

Spear

Pack and food

Dagger

Shield

Axe

Sword

Leather pad for protection

Woollen tunic

Leather sandals

● In warmer parts of the empire, soldiers didn't wear much under their tunics. But in chilly places they wore thick woollen underpants – just like the locals.

Who attacked the Romans with elephants?

Hannibal was the Spanish leader of the Carthaginians, a people from North Africa. He led a huge army and a herd of elephants across France and over the snow-covered Alps on a long march to Italy. In battle, the elephants charged at the Roman soldiers, who soon ran away in terror.

● Queen Cleopatra of Egypt used her beauty and charm to fight against the Romans. She made two Roman commanders fall in love with her – Julius Caesar and Mark Antony.

● In Britain the Romans built Hadrian's Wall, which was 120 kilometres long. From its towers, they spied on tribes in Scotland to the north.

● Forty thousand men and 37 elephants made the long, dangerous march from Spain across the Alps – the mountains in northern Italy. Sadly, many of them died from cold along the way.

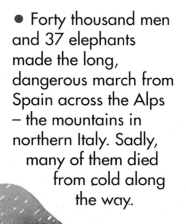

Which Roman guards went quack-quack-quack?

A flock of holy geese lived among the temples on Rome's Capitoline Hill. One dark night, a fierce tribe called the Gauls were planning an attack. They crept up the hill, but were heard by the geese, who quacked a loud warning and saved the citizens of Rome.

Who cut the Romans to pieces?

When the Romans attacked Britain, they had to face fierce warriors like Queen Boudicca. Legend says she fixed sharp knives to the wheels of her chariot and then drove right into the lines of soldiers. Ouch!

Who did the Romans worship?

The Romans worshipped hundreds of different gods and goddesses. They believed that the gods watched over them night and day. Some looked after the earth and the sea. Some cared for special groups such as doctors, merchants or soldiers. And others watched over the different parts of people's lives – their health, beauty or love life.

● The Romans thought that snakes brought good luck, so they painted them on their walls.

● The Romans believed that spirits lived in the rivers, woods and fields. They protected wild animals and the plants that grew there.

Jupiter, king of the gods

Mars, god of war

Venus, goddess of love

Juno, queen of the gods

• Sick Romans prayed to the gods to cure them. If they got better, they left a thank-you present in the temple – a little statue of the part of their body that had been cured.

Neptune, god of the sea

Diana, goddess of the Moon and of hunting

• The Romans built temples as homes for the gods. Each god or goddess had a temple of their own. It was built in the finest stone, and decorated with statues and carvings.

Apollo, god of the Sun and of the arts

Why did Romans jump in the bath together?

In Roman times, baths weren't just places to get clean. They were more like today's health clubs. People went there to keep fit, play games or sports, meet up with their friends, relax after a hard day's work – and give themselves a jolly good wash, too!

● The Romans hardly ever used soap – but they weren't dirty. They rubbed olive oil all over their skin, and then scraped it off with a blunt metal tool called a strigil. The dirt on their skin came off with the oil.

● Hot air from underground furnaces was used to heat the bath water. But it also made the bottom of the bath very hot, so some people wore sandals rather than burn their feet!

● Some public baths had a library – very handy for people who liked reading in the bath.

How many people could fit on the loo?

The Romans didn't go to the toilet on their own. Sometimes as many as 16 people sat side by side, laughing and chatting with one another. All of the cities had multi-seat public toilets. They were cheap to build, and easy to clean.

ENGAGED

● Most homes didn't have a toilet. Families used big pottery jars instead.

Who lived in high-rise flats?

Rome was a crowded city, and short of space. Most ordinary people lived in blocks of flats about six storeys high. On the ground floor were noisy shops and taverns. At the top were stuffy attic rooms. The nicest flats were somewhere in between.

● The Romans liked gardening. Rich people's gardens had pools and fountains. But even the poorest families kept flowerpots on the windowsill.

● Roman high-rises were so badly built that they often fell down. To stop the accidents, the Emperor Augustus passed a law forbidding any new building more than 20 metres high.

Which houses had holes in the roof?

Rich people's houses were built around an open-air courtyard. The open roof let in daylight and cool breezes during the summer – but chilly wind and rain in the winter.

Which guard dog was made of stone?

Many Roman homes had a picture of a guard dog near the front door. Like all mosaics, they were made of tiny pieces of stone. The words 'CAVE CANEM' (say *cah-vay cah-nem*) meant 'Beware of the dog' – to scare off any burglars!

Who brought slaves, spices and silk?

Merchants travelled to the very ends of the empire, and beyond, to bring back goods for the citizens of Rome.

As well as ordinary things like corn and timber, they brought slaves from North Africa, spices from India and beautiful silk from China.

● Ostia was the port of Rome. It lay on the coast, 25 kilometres from the city. Sacks of corn and jars of wine and olive oil were stored in warehouses at the port, and sent up to the market by barge.

● Most merchants preferred to keep their ships in port all winter, safe from storms and shipwrecks.

● To prevent traffic jams, traders and farmers could only bring their goods into Rome at night. With all those noisy carts, it must have been hard to sleep!

Where was the world's first shopping centre?

Trajan's Forum was a marketplace in Rome's city centre. It had 150 shops, brand new offices, and a huge open space where traders could set up their stalls. Citizens strolled around the Forum, looking at the goods and gossiping with their family and friends.

Who went to school in Roman times?

● Roman children only studied three subjects at junior school – reading, writing and sums.

Boys and girls from well-off families went to school when they were seven years old. But poor children stayed at home. Some of them ran errands for their parents or looked for work. Others played in the street and got into trouble.

What language did the Romans speak?

Everyone who lived in Italy spoke Latin. Everywhere else in the empire, people spoke their own local languages. But there were so many that people from different parts of the empire had to learn Latin, too, so that they could all understand one another!

- Girls left school at 11 but boys stayed on till they were 16 or 18 years old.

What did the children play with?

Roman children played with all sorts of odds and ends. If they couldn't afford glass or pottery marbles, they used little round nuts instead. They also threw dice made of bones. They even used pigs' bladders – blown up like balloons – to play football with!

CAESAR HORRIBILISSIMUS EST

- The Romans loved to scribble on walls. On many of their buildings you can still see the rude things they wrote about their leaders, enemies, and even their friends!

- The Romans used letters for numbers:
I was 1,
V was 5,
X was 10,
L was 50, and so on. Have you noticed the Roman page numbers in this book?

I, II, III, IV, V, VI, VII, VIII, IX, X, XI, XII, XIII, XIV...

Why were Roman roads so straight?

The Romans were brilliant engineers. Before they built a road, they used measuring instruments to work out where the road should go. They chose the shortest, straightest route between two camps, forts, or towns – and got rid of any hedges, buildings or other obstacles in the way. The roads linked the whole empire.

PLAN VIEW

SIDE ELEVATION

ARCHITECT
Marcus

● Road-builders put milestones along the side of the road so that travellers knew how far they had gone. A Roman mile was 1,000 paces long, about 1.6 kilometres.

ROME
500
MILES

● The roads had strong foundations. On the bottom, a thick layer of sand was covered first by stones, and then by gravel. On the top was a smooth surface of carefully-fitted paving stones.

Which bridges were always full of water?

Aqueducts look rather like bridges, but instead of a pathway along the top they have a deep channel of water. The Romans built them to carry water from mountain streams to nearby cities. Without aqueducts, the people wouldn't have had their baths, toilets or fountains of fresh running water.

CLAUDIUS
EMPEROR

IPPA II

● The Romans invented concrete by mixing lime, water and the ash from volcanoes. Concrete was as strong as stone, and it set hard even under water.

● The Romans invented arches, too. Each arch rested on a wooden frame until the very last stone, called the keystone, was in place.

Who was thrown to the lions?

● The amphitheatre in Rome was the Colosseum. It could seat up to 50,000 spectators.

On special days, people flocked to see spectacular shows at the amphitheatre. Christians, criminals and slaves were thrown into a ring with lions, and were chased, wounded and killed. The crowds cheered noisily. They thought it was fun to watch people suffer – but to us it seems wicked and cruel.

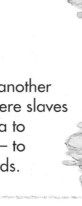

● Watching men fight was another popular sport. Gladiators were slaves who were sent into the arena to kill animals – or each other – to please the bloodthirsty crowds.

● Lions, leopards, crocodiles, wolves and bears – many different kinds of animal were shipped to Rome from all over the empire. Thousands were killed in the amphitheatre in a single day.

Were there hippos in the hippodrome?

The hippodrome, or circus, was a huge sports stadium with an oval-shaped racetrack. There were no hippos, but there were exciting chariot races. This was the Romans' favourite sport, and huge crowds filled the hippodrome to bet on their favourite teams.

Where can you visit a Roman town?

Pompeii was a bustling town not far from Rome. In the year AD 79, a nearby volcano erupted, and buried the town in ash. Pompeii lay hidden for centuries until, one day, some farmers discovered its Roman remains. Today you can visit to see what life was like in Roman times.

● Archaeologists have studied Pompeii since the 1800s, and have uncovered an almost-perfect Roman town.

MAKING MODELS

1 People were buried by the volcano's ash. Over the years, their bodies rotted away, leaving people-shaped holes in the hardened ash, or rock.

2 Archaeologists used the holes as moulds. They poured plaster inside, and waited for it to set.

3 Chipping away at the rock left plaster models of the Romans. Archaeologists study these carefully to learn about Roman life.

• Mount Vesuvius was an active volcano. As it erupted, showers of ash poured onto Pompeii, killing the people with poisonous fumes.

• The Roman empire grew weaker and weaker. It was attacked by warriors from the north and the east, who split up the empire into many small kingdoms.

How do we know about the Romans?

The Roman empire came to an end in the 470s. Yet Roman buildings, mosaics, writings, paintings and weapons have all survived. Remains like these tell us about the people and the way they lived.

• Some Roman finds are rather peculiar. Archaeologists in London have dug up a pair of black leather knickers. Who could have lost them all those years ago?

Index

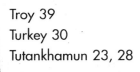